THE
Archive Photographs
SERIES

AROUND
PORT TALBOT
AND ABERAVON

The chapter-house at Margam Abbey in 1887, the remains of a once magnificent Cistercian architectural masterpiece, the construction of which started in 1147.

THE
Archive Photographs
SERIES

AROUND PORT TALBOT AND ABERAVON

Compiled by
Keith E. Morgan

TEMPUS

First published 1997
Copyright © Keith E. Morgan, 1997

The Chalford Publishing Company
St Mary's Mill, Chalford,
Stroud, Gloucestershire, GL6 8NX

ISBN 0 7524 0608 6

Typesetting and origination by
The Chalford Publishing Company
Printed in Great Britain by
Bailey Print, Dursley, Gloucestershire

Cover illustration
Mansel Tinplate Works engineering department, 1903. (See page 22)

On his first solo attempt of the Mumbles to Aberavon annual swim in September 1963, Bernard Donovan of Aberavon (third from the left), was accompanied by three generations of swimmers: Cyril Jenkins (far right) who held the pre-war record after his 1939 swim; Dick Landeg (second from left) who restarted the Mumbles to Aberavon annual swim in 1960, and who for many years organised and captained the Aberavon Swimming Club water-polo team; and Charlie Taylor (first on left) who dominated the Mumbles to Aberavon swim during the 1960s. Mr Donovan's completed time for the 1963 swim, was clocked at 3 hours 43 minutes by Arthur Cleary, the official timekeeper. The first Mumbles to Aberavon swim was held on 22 September 1928 and was accomplished by Charlie Lucas and Ted Tuck. Lucas's time was 5 hours 44 minutes.

Mr and Mrs George and Sarah Gibbs, with daughter Evelyn, and baby Kate in the perambulator, out walking in Baglan Road near St Catherine's Church, Baglan, c. 1900.

Contents

Councillor T.D. Melvin John, Mayor of Neath Port Talbot County Borough Council, 1997–98
(photograph by Eric Rees, ABIPP, Swansea).

Foreword

By Cllr T.D. Melvin John, Mayor of Neath Port Talbot County Borough Council (1997–98)

It is a great pleasure to introduce this collection of archive photographs of Port Talbot. The book is one of a series of such volumes featuring South Wales towns, published by Chalford. Appropriately, this particular volume has been published in 1997, the year in which Margam Abbey marked the 850th anniversary of its foundation, and St Theodore's Church in Port Talbot celebrated its centenary.

The volume encompasses an area extending from Baglan in the west, to Margam in the east, and north from Aberavon to Pontrhydyfen. It will therefore be of great interest to people from a wide area. Keith Morgan, the compiler, has collected photographs from many sources, both public and private, and is to be congratulated on his thorough and meticulous research which has resulted in the unearthing of much previously unpublished material. Thus, the volume complements the fine series *Old Port Talbot and District in Photographs* published by the Port Talbot Historical Society during recent years.

The contents of the book have been grouped into subjects which reflect many aspects of the history of the town and the surrounding area, including maritime activity, education, religion, sport, and its important industrial heritage. I commend the book as one which will be of great interest both to residents of Port Talbot and Aberavon, and to visitors to the area.

Acknowledgements

As with the two previous books that I have had the privilege to compile in the *Archive Photographs* series, the response that I have received has been enthusiastic and overwhelming. Again, the list of individuals, professional photographers, and organisations which have provided photographs and given information appeared at times to be endless and I am always concerned that I might miss someone out in this list of acknowledgements. If I have, it is entirely unintentional.

The production of this book has been made possible by the following whose help and co-operation I would duly and sincerely like to acknowledge:

Revd Colin Amos, Mr and Mrs Ridian Angell, Mrs Jacqueline Bate, Ms Susan Beckley, Revd Derek Belcher, Mr and Mrs John Blundell, Mr David Carrington, Mrs Pauline Clarke, Mr Mike Cliff, Mr Ray Cottrell, Mr and Mrs Colin Davies, Mr and Mrs Gerwyn Davies, Mrs Janet Davies, Mr Les Davies, Mr Lyn Lewis Davies, Mr Bernard Donovan, Mr Gareth Dowdell, Mr Lloyd Ellis, Mr and Mrs Laurie Evans, the late Mr Leslie Evans, Mrs Binnie Felton, Mr David Fletcher; Ms Rosalyn Gee, Miss Beryl George, Mr and Mrs Ernest Griffiths, Mr and Mrs Jeffrey Groom, Miss Terry Hill, Mr Paul Hinder; Mr John Vivian Hughes, Mr Graham Jenkins, Cllr and Mrs T.D. Melvin John, Mrs Donna Jones, Mr J.I. Stuart Joseph, Mr Peter Kidd, Mr and Mrs Peter Knowles, Mr (the late) and Mrs Gerard Lahive, Revd David Lewis, Mr and Mrs Tony Llewellyn, Mr and Mrs David Murphy, Revd and Mrs H.E. Osmar, Mr and Mrs Syd Parry, Mr and Mrs John Poston, Mrs Rene Poston, Mr and Mrs Arthur Rees, the late Mr Bert Ridd, Mr and Mrs Ron Ridd, Mrs Margaret Roddis, Ms Jennifer Sabine, Mr Ken Sawyer, Mr and Mrs Barry Stephens, Mr and Mrs Peter Stevens, Mr Hywel Thomas, Mr and Mrs Barry Warner.

Aberavon Rugby Football Club; British Steel plc, Strip Products, Port Talbot; Glamorgan-Gwent Archaeological Trust; Kenfig National Nature Reserve; Kenfig Society; Margam Cricket Club; National Library of Wales, Aberystwyth; Neath Port Talbot County Borough Council: Leisure Services, Library and Information Services, Mayoral and Civic Services; Peter Knowles, photographer; Port Talbot Historical Society; Science Museum, London; Swansea Museum; Tank Museum, Bovington Camp, Wareham; West Glamorgan Archive Service.

I would especially like to thank the Mayor of Neath Port Talbot County Borough Council, Cllr Mel John, for writing the Foreword and for giving me his support in this venture. My thanks are also extended to the Neath Port Talbot County Borough Council Library and Information Service, the West Glamorgan Archive Service, the Port Talbot Historical Society and Peter Knowles, photographer, for their help and for allowing me free access to their photographic collections. I would also like to extend my gratitude to Mr Simon Eckley, my editor and mentor, for guiding me along the tricky path that eventually leads to publication. Finally, I would like to acknowledge the support and patience of my wife Malvina and to thank her for proof-reading and checking the contents of the book.

Introduction

In producing this book, the Chalford Publishing Company has given me the opportunity to present for general pleasure, 230 or so old photographs of Port Talbot, Aberavon and the surrounding area. Throughout its compilation, I have been conscious of the fact that the Port Talbot Historical Society has already produced four very fine volumes in their *Old Port Talbot & District in Photographs* series. Even though this series is of a similar nature to that of the current publication, I have tried wherever possible to use different material. Nevertheless, the Port Talbot Historical Society has kindly allowed me to use some photographs from its earlier and now-out-of-print volumes where it has been necessary for me to illustrate a point or provide continuity to a theme. I was again very fortunate to be given access to a number of private albums from which I have been able to select many unique photographs. It will be the first time that some of the prints from these collections have been seen outside an immediate family circle. Likewise, I have received photographs from a number of organisations who have either allowed me to draw from their archives or who have secured prints for me to include in this book.

The layout of the book follows the pattern that I have adopted for my previous publications where I try in the first chapter to give the reader a feel for the history of the area being covered. For obvious reasons, photographic coverage of events has only been possible since the mid-1800s when cameras first came into use. I have been fortunate in being able to include some of the earliest photographs taken in Wales by the pioneer of photography William Henry Fox Talbot, and by his Welsh contemporaries, Revd Calvert Jones and John Dillwyn Llewellyn. I have also tried to bring history to life by reproducing old drawings and maps and by using modern photographs to illustrate an interesting subject. The reader will notice that some of the prints in this book are of a fairly recent date. Working on the principle that today is the history of tomorrow, I have made every effort to capture events as they have occurred because I know that by the time this book is published they will have already become a memory.

In this year of publication, 1997, there are a number of celebratory events taking place in the district to which I have tried to give appropriate coverage in this book. Notably, we have the 850th anniversary of the foundation of Margam Abbey, the 125th anniversary of the founding of the Margam Cricket Club, the centenary of the opening and consecration of St Theodore's Church, the 50th anniversary of both the Port Talbot & District Amateur Operatic Society and the incorporation of the Steel Company of Wales as a company and the start of construction at the £73 million Abbey Works. There are also several other organisations and occasions which are featured as they form part of the rich heritage of the area. Among these, and to name but a few, are: Aberavon RFC (the 'Wizards'), formed in 1876; St Joseph's Green Stars RFC which first came into existence in the late 1880s; Glan Afan (Port Talbot County) School which celebrated its centenary in 1996; the Port Talbot and Aberavon Amateur Operatic Society, in existence now for some seventy-odd years; the Mumbles to Aberavon Swim which first took place in 1928; and the Cwmavon Philharmonic Glee Club which was certainly well established by 1929. An event also of significance in such an ancient borough is that the youngest-ever mayor of Port Talbot, Cllr Mel John, is now Mayor of Neath Port Talbot County Borough Council for 1997–98. I would like to take this opportunity to offer him and his Lady Mayoress wife Barbara, every best wishes for their year in office and trust that this book, *Around Port Talbot and Aberavon*, will serve both them and every other reader as a suitable pictorial souvenir of our times.

The author on top of the remains of the Second-World-War radar station on Mynydd Margam. This was an ideal spot for such an installation with the location offering a clear and unobstructed view in all directions.

One
Historical Background

There was a glacier on your doorstep! A view of Craig Avon, Corlannau, from the M4 motorway at Aberavon. Mynydd Emroch, on the right of the photograph, is over 210m (690ft) high, while Mynydd Dinas, on the other side of the valley, is 258m (846ft) above sea-level at its highest point. The outline of Foel Fynyddau (370m or 1,214ft high at its peak) can be seen in the distance brooding over Pontrhydyfen. This landscape was largely formed under ice (which began a final retreat from Wales about 10,000 BC). The large sheets of ice that had covered the surface of the earth with a blanket sometimes many hundreds of metres thick, retreated northwards exposing the land mass as we more or less recognise it today. Over many thousands of years, a great glacier had carved out the characteristic deep U-shape of the present Afan valley. The glacier would have towered some 200m (656ft) above a present-day onlooker standing in Velindre and its face would have stretched right across the mouth of the valley. When it receded about 14,000 years ago, the glacier deposited at the limit of its forward movement a small mountain of rubble – a terminal moraine – known locally as Craig Avon. It is over 60m (197ft) high and is made up of a mass of rocks, gravel, and sand gouged out of the mountain-sides by the glacier as it slowly edged its way forward to form the Afan valley. When the ice melted, the river Afan was formed and it cut a deep channel through the glacial deposit at Craig Avon as it made its way through to the sea. A similar geological effect can also be seen in the nearby Goytre valley.

Four mid-Bronze Age axes found at Morfa Beach by John Player in March 1988. As the ice sheets melted and the glaciers retreated north, so the sea-level began to slowly rise. The Bristol Channel was formed and the sea reached the Port Talbot area about 8,900 years ago penetrating further inland beyond the present coastline. Thick marine deposits gradually accumulated and periods of storms caused the formation of sand dunes along the coastline until the low-lying areas of Aberavon and Margam Moors became land about 3,500 years ago. Indications are that early man had settled in the area by the Neolithic period (4,500–2,500 BC). Habitation would have started as isolated homesteads with possibly the existence of a settlement at Aberavon before and during Roman times. Such a settlement would have been very busy during the Roman era as witnessed by the great number of Roman remains found in the area, especially when the new dock was being constructed at the turn of the century.

The Maximinus stone, now to be seen at the Margam Stones Museum. This Roman milestone is one of four which have been discovered in the area. It is of Rhaetic sandstone and was found in 1839 on the former route of the main A48 road near the old toll-cottage in Tollgate Road, Margam. It was broken into five fragments of which one piece is missing. The stone had been used on two separate occasions, first as a milestone and then to mark an early Christian burial. The original inscription commemorates two Roman emperors: Maximinus Daia, named Caesar in AD 305, and Augustus who succeeded him four years later. The stone was erected between AD 309 and the death of Augustus in AD 313. In the sixth century, the stone was reused by one Paulinus as a Christian memorial to his son Cantusus.

A brass sestertius coin of Titus Caesar, AD 77–78. The obverse (*left*) shows the head of Titus Caesar while the figure of Roma is depicted on the reverse (*right*). This first-century coin, in remarkable condition, was found by local historian Gerard Lahive on Morfa Beach in September 1990. It is one of a number of coins found that adds to the evidence of a strong Roman presence in the area.

The carved sixth-century stone found by Gerard Lahive, near Eglwys Nunydd, Margam, July 1992. Mr Lahive is seen here inspecting the incised stone with Steven Sell, finds officer of the Glamorgan-Gwent Archaeological Trust. The stone was uncovered by members of Roadforce West Glamorgan as they renewed street lighting on Water Street, which follows the course of the old Roman road which led from Margam to North Cornelly. The stone is thought to be part of a much larger decorated monument, similar to exhibits in the Margam Stones Museum.

The author (left), with Jacqueline Bate and Malvina Morgan (right) at the Boduoc stone, Mynydd Margam. The original is on display in the Margam Stones Museum. On 23 April 1994 members of the Kenfig Society repeated the walk made by the Cardiff Naturalists' Society in 1895 over the mountain from Margam to this stone. A translation of the lettering, which is in debased Roman capitals and indicates a date in the sixth century, reads: 'Here lies Boduoc, son of Cattegern, great-grandson of Eternalis Vedomavus'.

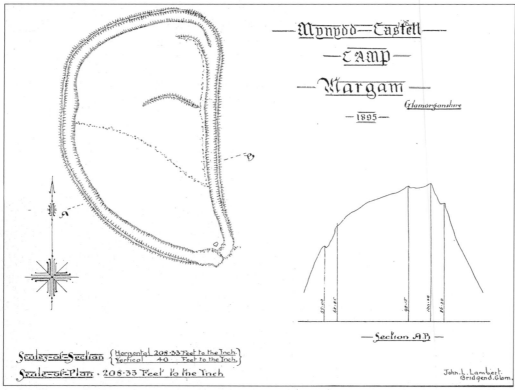

Mynydd Castell Camp at Margam as recorded by the archaeological section of the Cardiff Naturalists' Society in 1895. This Iron Age fort stood sentinel over the coastal plain extending past Mynydd Margam and beyond to the west.

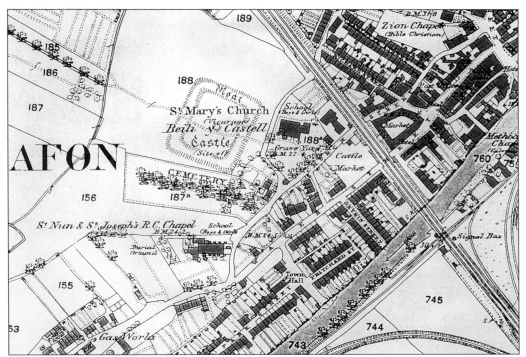

This plan of Aberavon Castle (centre left), which is taken from the first edition of the 25in to 1 mile Ordnance Survey map (Glamorgan sheet XXV 13), is the only known depiction of the castle that appears to be in existence. It gradually crumbled into ruin and, in 1895, the demolished walls were used to fill in the moat prior to urban development taking place. Just one relic remains – a salvaged stone which can be seen at Margam Abbey. Probably built by Caradog, Welsh lord of Afan, the castle occupied a well-chosen position. Not only did it provide control over the ford crossing the river, but its position would have denied access to and from the west via the narrow coastal plain as well as securing the gateway to the Afan valley.

Castle Street, Aberavon. The castle was located centrally in the photograph, just below the flyover between St Joseph's Church on the left and St Mary's Church on the right.

In the porch of St Mary's Church, Aberavon is reputed to be the headstone for the grave of Thomas, rector of Avene (d. 1350), who drew up the original charter of Afan. The slab measures 1.68m by 0.61m (5ft 6in by 2ft) and has an incised Calvary cross from top to bottom. Just below the left arm of the cross is a chalice and under this the sign of episcopal authority – crossed keys.

'The actual "chopping block" used as a secret hiding place for the original charter of Aberavon Borough.' This rough block of oak is on display in the reception hall of the Civic Centre at Port Talbot. The block has a six-inch-deep cavity, originally disguised by a hinged cover now partly rotted away. The iron hinges are of a typical seventeenth-century design and the block has also been reinforced with iron bars, together with a loop which was probably secured with a padlock. Legend has it that this block was used by the portreeve to hide the town charters from Oliver Cromwell. The townsfolk had evidently showed Royalist sympathies, and in order to ensure the safety of the charters, the portreeve hid them in the cavity and continued chopping wood on the block when Cromwell's emissaries demanded their surrender!

The remains of a monastic grange found during the construction of the Abbey Steelworks on Morfa Moors, February 1949. The two sections of the exposed stone walling and internal stone staircase were inspected by Dr Iorwerth C. Peate, keeper of the Welsh Folk Museum at St Fagans, together with Dr Nash-Williams and Professor William Rees of the University College of Cardiff. These experts expressed the opinion that the remains were probably from a grange of Margam Abbey. Later investigations indicated that the ruin was of the Terries Grange which was eventually abandoned in the sixteenth century due to the encroaching sand. Thomas Gray, the historian, had previously discovered and reported on these monastic remains as far back as 1898.

This stark outline against the sky is all that remains of what was possibly the Hermitage of St Theodoric, British Steel's Abbey Works, Port Talbot, May 1993.

Two early views of Margam Castle taken by Fox Talbot, *c.* 1940. ?
Above: part of the south front and tower; *below*: the corner of the south-west wing. William Henry Fox Talbot, the pioneer of many techniques of photography, was the cousin of Christopher Rice Mansel Talbot of Margam Castle, and he visited the Talbot family on numerous occasions. The originals of both these photographs are held at the Science Museum in London.

The earliest-known photograph by a Welshman, a daguerreotype of Margam Castle, taken in 1841 by Swansea clergyman Calvert R. Jones when construction of the castle was still unfinished. For many years, the photograph hung at Margam Castle. It came to light again in November 1987 when it was offered for sale at Sotheby's. The National Library of Wales was outbid by an American Gallery, but the following year the Library won an appeal against an export licence and bought the photograph for £20,000.

The orangery at Margam photographed c. 1850 by John Dillwyn Llewellyn, another Welsh pioneer photographer who was born in Penllergare, Glamorgan. Much respected in his own time by his fellow photographers, John Dillwyn Llewellyn was a founder member in 1853 of the Photographic Society. The original of the above photograph is held by the National Library of Wales.

Carrying on in the true spirit of pioneer Fox Talbot and his contemporaries, Peter Knowles, a professional photographer from Port Talbot, took this dramatic picture of Margam Castle during the disastrous fire that engulfed the building on 4 August 1977. The fire completely destroyed the inside of the castle and it is only in recent years that the building has been restored to its former glory.

Peter Knowles outside his photographic shop in Talbot Road, Port Talbot. The business was first started by Peter's father, Vivian Knowles, who was employed as a sign-writer with the Western Welsh Bus Company before the Second World War. He served with the RAF and on demob, he returned to his old job for a short period. Vivian bought his first camera in 1947 for 5/- and promptly went into the photographic business. He died in December 1996, aged 86 leaving a widow Mary (May). Peter Knowles started taking photographs when he was eighteen and eventually took over the running of the business which is still going strong. Many of the photographs reproduced in this book are from the cameras of Vivian and Peter Knowles.

Two

Industry

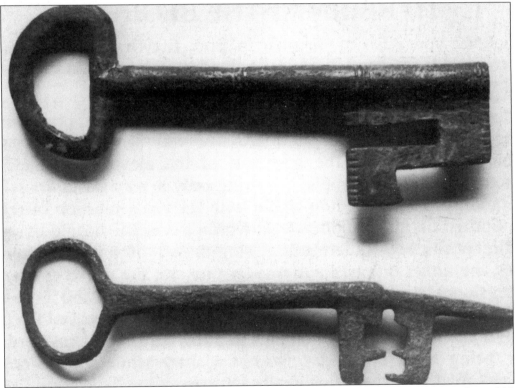

Industry of one sort or another has been carried on in this area for many centuries. Over 800 years ago, the monks of Margam Abbey mined coal via a shaft dug into the sandstone of Mynydd Margam. At the same time, local farmers were extracting small quantities of coal for their domestic needs, direct from outcrops. Other forms of industry were also carried out as evidenced by the two medieval iron keys shown in the above photograph. They were found during construction of the Abbey Steel Works in February 1947, at the same time as the Terries Grange shown on page 17 was rediscovered. The bottom key is probably fifteenth-century while the top key dates from the thirteenth century and is more significant in that it bears traces of a tin coating.

The engineering department of the Mansel Tinplate Works, Aberavon, *c.* 1891. The gearbox in the foreground bears a cast-iron plate which carries the lettering 'R.B. Byass & Co., Margam, 1891'. George Henry Gibbs is standing second from the left in the photograph, behind the little boy in the shaft of the toothed wheel.

Mansel Tinplate Works engineering department, 1903. In this view, George Henry Gibbs is sitting fourth from the right.

A pre-Second-World-War view taken from Mynydd Margam looking out over Morfa Moors. The old toll-gate cottage (demolished in 1955), Tollgate Road, Margam, can just be distinguished in the centre of the photograph. The old stone bridge crossing the GWR main railway line was demolished to make way for a new steel bridge when the Abbey Works was being built at the beginning of the 1950s.

'Morfa Colliery, Glamorganshire, scene of the late fatal colliery explosion.' An artist from the *Illustrated London News* visited the scene of the dramatic accident which occurred in 1863, and while he was sketching at the pit's mouth the search for the 39 men who lost their lives was still being pursued. Note the coffins held in readiness in the building on the left. The shaft for the Morfa Colliery was sunk in 1847–49 by Messrs Vivian & Company, owners of the Taibach Copper Works. The mine workings extended well out under the sea off Morfa Beach.

The unveiling in March 1990 of a memorial to the miners who lost their lives in explosions at Morfa Colliery between 1849 and 1890. About a hundred people, including members of the Port Talbot Historical Society who had instigated the idea of erecting a memorial, watched the ceremony. Joan James, on the far right of the photograph, is the great-granddaughter of the under-manager, William Cuthbert Barrass, who was killed with 86 other miners in the last explosion of 1890. His body was not recovered until five years later and identified then only by his miner's lamp which Mrs James is holding. The colliery reopened after the 1890 accident, but eventually closed down permanently in September 1913.

An aerial view of the Abbey Works of the Steel Company of Wales Ltd while under construction *c.* 1948. The plant occupied the greater part of what had been previously the marshland and sand dunes of Morfa Moors. By June 1960, it was one of the largest integrated steelworks in Europe and covered 1,000 acres along 4.5 miles of the South Wales coast. It was a 'city of steel' where 17,000 people worked around the clock, with its own power-houses, bus services, catering facilities, and railway station.

The general offices of the Abbey Works, early 1950s.

Due to the illness of King George VI, who was due to open the new Abbey Works, the ceremony was performed in July 1951 by the Chancellor of the Exchequer, the Rt Hon Hugh Gaitskell MP. The above photograph was taken of guests and members of staff at that time. From left to right: O.G. Daniel, Megan Williams, -?-, Etty Parry, Lulu Haines, Terresa O'Donovan, Binnie McNeil, -?-, Terry Hill, Bessy Llewellyn, Kitty Edwards, Tom ?, Joyce Edwards, -?-, -?-, Cyril Havard, Margaret Jones, Winnie Morgan, Arthur Roberts, Sister Anne Haycock, Marion Jones, -?-.

Abbey Works' hallo girls in 1957. From left to right, standing: Hilda Williams (supervisor), Lil Cound, -?-; seated: Joyce Luckwell, Evelyn Elward, Val Care, Malvina Angell, Vera Denner. The switchboard was a GPO PMBX (private manual branch exchange) model 1A. This was used for all external calls. The Abbey Works also had its own separate and completely independent automatic telephone exchange with communication cover extending right throughout the plant.

The main staff canteen at the Abbey Works in the early 1950s. There were a number of other canteens built throughout the works and equipped with modern kitchens to cater for the needs of the work force. All catering facilities were provided in-house.

Three heroines of the January 1982 'snow siege' at the Abbey Works. On three consecutive days, Morwen Pugh (left), Thelma Morgans (centre), and Angela Jones, trudged about a mile through knee-deep snow to get to work, and for shifts of 12 hours each they cooked for the beleaguered men. No wonder they topped the works' popularity charts at the time.

A typical scene at the Abbey Works during the clean-up after the exceptionally heavy snow storm of January 1982.

Crowds of well-wishers waiting at the Taibach entrance to the Port Talbot Works in order to greet the Queen and the Duke of Edinburgh on their arrival for the opening of the giant new harbour and basic-oxygen-steel-making plant, Tuesday, 12 May 1970.

The Queen and the Duke of Edinburgh driving past works' employees on their way through Port Talbot Works to open the British Steel Corporation's new basic-oxygen-steel-making plant, Tuesday, 12 May 1970.

Port Talbot Works' employees and others lining the route that the Queen and the Duke of Edinburgh would be following on their way to the new harbour.

The Queen performing the opening ceremony of the British Transport Dock Board's new deep-water harbour at Port Talbot, on Tuesday, 12 May 1970. The international sundial in front of the Queen was calibrated to show the time both at Port Talbot and in some of the major ports throughout the world. It has remained as a permanent memorial to Her Majesty's visit.

The Queen and royal party walking past the crowd of guests and onlookers lining the foreshore after she had opened the new deep-water tidal harbour at Port Talbot.

The Queen and the Duke of Edinburgh driving along the jetty of the new deep-water harbour at Port Talbot. The royal inauguration of the £20 million British Transport Docks Board's tidal harbour and British Steel's new £18 million basic-oxygen-steel-making plant, put the Port Talbot Works back amongst the industrial forerunners of the world.

Striking steel workers from British Steel Corporation's Panteg Works marching through Port Talbot, 1980.

Not long after the steel workers' strike was resolved, the miners went on strike throughout the country. Here members of the Penrhiwceiber and Tower lodges of the NUM are seen marching through Port Talbot, 1980.

A summer welcome of real warmth and affection greeted Prince Charles and Princess Diana when they arrived at Port Talbot on 11 June 1986 to officially open the works' recently modernised hot-strip mill. Princess Diana acknowledges the cheers of employees. Looking on are Prince Charles; John Madden (Port Talbot Works director), and Arthur Bowden (manager of works operations).

Cllr Mel John, Mayor of Neath Port Talbot County Borough Council for 1997–98, was installed with due ceremony on 16 May 1997. Peter Kidd (director of British Steel Integrated Works) is pictured making presentations both to the new mayor and the immediate past mayor, Roy Jones (left). Cllr John was a Port Talbot Works employee for 34 years before taking early retirement in 1982. In 1959 he won the ward election for Cwmavon and at 25 became the youngest Port Talbot councillor. He subsequently became the youngest mayor of Port Talbot in 1971–72 at 39. He was elected chairman of West Glamorgan County Council in 1986–87 and, with his present appointment, he has achieved a rare treble by serving on three different councils.

Three

The Sea

Long before the development that has taken place over the last hundred or so years, the sea featured prominently in the history of this stretch of coastline. From the finds made along the beach extending from Briton Ferry to Sker Point at Porthcawl, evidence has been found to show that ancient man frequented the seashore. The Romans were great sailors and probably landed troops and supplies near the mouth of the river Afan during their occupation of South Wales. Later, in medieval times, Aberavon must have been a port of some significance to have a portreeve. This was an important civic position in the town until 1860 when the title was changed to mayor. The sea has not always been of a beneficial nature, however. Flooding and the encroachment of sand has taken place many times over the centuries and the coastline is littered with the wrecks of unfortunate vessels. Legend would have us believe that there are sunken treasure ships from the Spanish Armada waiting to be discovered on Morfa and Kenfig sands. The coin shown in the above photographs, a Spanish four reals minted in Mexico 1536–72, was found on Morfa Beach by Gerard Lahive and probably came from a sunken British cargo vessel. There was considerable trade with Spain around this period and payments for the delivered merchandise would have been made with such coinage.

Reflections in the still water around the wreck of the *Michael Swenden* which was driven ashore on Aberavon sands in February 1957. Such sights were once commonplace along this stretch of coastline. One shipwreck, that of the *Brodlands*, while being broken up by the borough engineer's department in June 1961, revealed steel-plate bearing the stamp of the old Port Talbot Steelworks! The *Brodlands* had run aground during a storm in January 1913.

Wrecks on the beach have not just been confined to ships. This mysterious stranded giant, a huge steel corkscrew over 60ft long, at least 10ft in diameter, and with an estimated weight of some 30 tonnes, was washed up on Morfa Beach in January 1990. It was identified as a giant auger or Archimedes screw which had been destined for Athens for use in a sewage treatment works there. It had fallen off the deck of a Dutch ship on 19 December 1989. However, because the captain thought that it had sunk, he did not bother to tell anyone, but merely entered it in the log book as missing. The auger was later spotted off the Cornish coast and because of its massive bulk and low profile in the water, coastguards and the Royal Navy gave regular radio broadcasts warning of the dangerous hazard presented to shipping by the bobbing object.

Port Talbot harbour, *c.* 1890, with a sailing ship taking on a cargo of coal from one of the coal-loading hoists and chutes. The photographs on this and the following page, are taken from an album of photographs of Port Talbot dock and railways covering the period from *c.* 1890 to 1910, which is held by the West Glamorgan County Archive Service (ref: D/D Z 276).

A dredger at work clearing the channel to Port Talbot Docks, *c.* 1900.

The old south breakwater to Port Talbot Dock, together with the new one under construction, *c.* 1890.

The lock gates to the newly constructed deep-water dock at Port Talbot, opened in 1890. As a result of the more sheltered situation offered by this deep-water harbour and that opened at Barry the previous year, Porthcawl harbour lost a major proportion of its coal-handling trade and was forced to close in 1903.

Christopher Rice Mansel Talbot's RYS (Royal Yacht Squadron) *Lynx*. One of the first sea voyages of this new yacht was to take Talbot, together with members of his family and distinguished guests, to the opening of the Suez Canal in 1869. The *Lynx* was a yacht of 564 tons, painted white, black and gold, and it was to serve Talbot for over two decades being used by the Prince and Princess of Wales on their visit to Swansea in 1881. Following Talbot's death in 1890, the *Lynx* was sold to E.T. Brown and Company for £650.

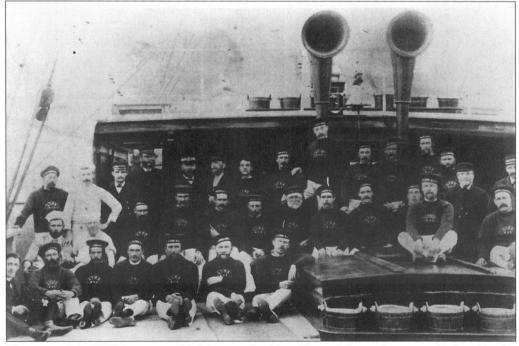

The crew of the RYS *Lynx*, *c.* 1881. Margaret Roddis of Port Talbot, whose grandfather Charles Rogers (fifth from the left in the back row) was captain of the *Lynx*, recalls that on one occasion, when he was taken ill, Emily Talbot visited him at his home in Margam Terrace, Port Talbot.

A reflective view of the old dock at Port Talbot with an iron-ore bulk carrier being discharged at the quayside by an ore-unloader transporter crane, pre-1970.

The giant *Forth Bridge*, with a cargo of 46,410 tons of iron ore from Port Cartier, Canada. Other than the *Orotava Bridge* iron-ore carrier that was used for berthing trials in January 1970, the *Forth Bridge* was the first ship to enter Port Talbot's £20 million tidal harbour in April 1970. She is shown here being guided to her berth on the new jetty by the motor tug *Mumbles*. This tug, the flagship of the Alexandra Towing Company, was specially built for the job of berthing the giant ore carriers in the new harbour. Launched in 1968, she is a forecastle-deck-type tug with an all-welded hull, 34m (112ft) long, and powered by British-built diesel engines that can develop up to 2,190 bhp.

An aerial view of the British Transport Dock Board's new deep-water harbour at Port Talbot looking south-east, 14 February 1970. It was the first new harbour to be built in Britain this century and accommodated the first iron-ore terminal capable of berthing and unloading giant ships of 100,000 tons and over. To stabilise the dredged-out, deep-water basin of the harbour, a firm of specialists was engaged to use an ancient fenlands craft that had started many centuries ago in Holland. A team of fifteen men covered the 35,000 square yards of the harbour bed with a 2ft-thick mattress of specially-bound willow reeds. In 1996, further dredging work was carried out in the tidal harbour to give British Steel an extra 2.5 million tonne capacity and to open up the harbour to commercial traffic as well.

Construction underway in 1968 on the north-west breakwater of the new deep-water tidal harbour at Port Talbot. Nearly 3.5 million tons of rock were used for the construction of the two breakwaters, most of it brought to the site from the quarries at Cornelly by 35-ton Caterpillar dump trucks via a specially constructed 9-mile haul road behind the sand dunes fronting the sea at Kenfig. The huge stones used for the breakwaters ranged in size from 40lb to 8 tons in weight.

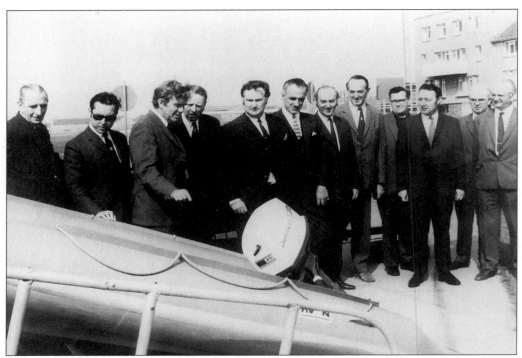

The Mayor of Port Talbot, Cllr Mel John, with Commander Thompson, inspecting the Royal National Lifeboat Institute's first inshore lifeboat to be stationed at Aberavon, 1971.

This mounted salmon on display in the Civic Centre, Aberavon, was caught by Colin Walton on 4 September 1988, and weighed in at 4lb 6oz. It was presented to Cllr Graham Jones, Leader of Port Talbot Borough Council, by the Afan Valley Angling Club. It was the first salmon to be caught in the river Afan for 150 years following many years of extensive environmental work carried out along the river length. There is a legend concerning the sacred salmon of Afan which is reputed to have appeared by Aberavon bridge on Christmas Day morning over many centuries and was so tame that it allowed local people to stroke it.

Four
Commerce and Trade

High Street, Aberavon, *c.* 1910, long before the days when busy traffic started passing through the town. In addition to the crowd of onlookers, the picture contains much information. Manchester House and the Temple of Fashion were housed in the buildings on the left. These were later to become Hodges and Lewis's, respectively. On the right is A. Watkiss, family butcher. Aberavon Council (Mountain) School can be seen in the centre background.

The scene at the new market, Aberavon, during the official laying of the two foundation stones, 1908. One was laid by the mayor, Henry Walsh JP, while the other was laid by his immediate successor, William Williams.

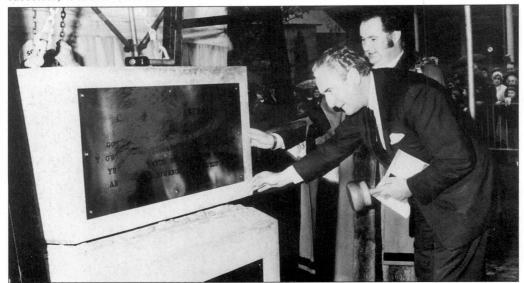

The Rt Hon Peter Thomas QC, MP, Secretary of State for Wales, lays the foundation stone for the new Aberafan Centre in the presence of the Mayor of Port Talbot, Alderman T.D. Melvyn John, Friday, 5 November 1971. Mr Thomas was invited to perform the ceremony by Cyril B. Leigh FRICS, managing director of Star Dolphin Development Ltd which developed the Aberafan Centre in conjunction with the Municipal Borough of Port Talbot. The completed centre was opened by HRH The Princess Anne on Friday, 20 February 1976.

Lloyds Bank is prominent on the street corner in this late 1930s photograph of Station Road, Port Talbot. Further down the road on the right-hand side at the next junction, the Midland Bank is just recognisable. In May 1958, this made the headlines with an attempted robbery. An empty shop opposite the bank was used by would-be robbers to dig a tunnel under the main road in an effort to reach the bank's vaults. After several days and nights of observation, the police raided the shop and arrested two men. Inside the shop, the police found several tons of earth piled high in the back of the premises. They also recovered picks, shovels, scoops and lighting equipment from underground excavations that had been dug to a depth of several feet under the building and main road.

J.H. Penhallurick's sweet shop in Station Road, Port Talbot, c. 1924. The premises are now occupied by Tom Phillips's electrical shop. The young lad sitting in the peddle car in the shop porch is Ron Ridd (now living in Cimla, Neath), who was about four years old at the time.

Minella's millinery shop, Bethany Square, Port Talbot, c. 1983. Margaret Minns started the business from a shop in the High Street area of town in 1963. Redevelopment of the town centre, with the subsequent demolition of these premises, necessitated a move to the present location. Since Mrs Minns retired in the early 1980s, the shop has been run by her daughter, Eleanor Dodd, who had always helped her mother in the business. Nowadays, shops dealing exclusively with the sale of headwear and matching accessories are few and far between. There was, however, an upsurge in the wearing of hats in the 1980s when the Princess of Wales started something of a fashion with her stylish choice of headgear. 'Lady Diana' hats became the rage of both young and the not-so-young. Today, Minnella's is the only hat shop in the Port Talbot centre area and concentrates on hat hire.

R. Daycock & Son, saddler's and riding equipment shop, Taibach, 1997. This traditional saddler's shop is currently run by Neil Daycock. The original business was started in 1948 by Arthur Daycock, with his father Roy, when he came out of the Army at the end of the Second World War. The original shop was at 35 Talbot Square. Two years later the business moved to a shop in Cwmavon Road, then in 1973 to its present location.

Left: the Walnut Tree Hotel, *c.* 1910. *Right*: Revd D.G. Belcher, vicar of Margam, in the Abbot's Kitchen at Margam Abbey, carrying on the catering tradition that was first started by the Cistercian monks who built the Abbey in 1147. Margam was the first of the cathedrals, abbeys, and greater churches in Wales to provide such a catering facility. Today, training courses are run in the Abbot's Kitchen for the hotel catering industry. With a background in dietetics and catering, and prior to going back to college to study for the priesthood, Revd Belcher worked as a state-registered dietician. He is qualified as a trainer and assessor for the National Vocational Qualification (NVQ).

The Twelve Knights Hotel, Margam, built to cater for the trade arising from the new Abbey Works of the Steel Company of Wales, was officially opened for business in the summer of 1957. The hotel was named after the legend of the 'Twelve Norman Knights of Glamorgan'. After the conquest of lowland Glamorgan was completed in the 1090s under the leadership of Sir Robert Fitzhammo, he is reputed to have met his knights and their esquires on a stretch of road outside Bridgend and paid them in gold as a reward for their services. This length of road is called 'The Golden Mile' to this day.

Members of Port Talbot Borough Council together with corresponding visiting dignitaries from the twin-town of Heilbronn, Germany, 1971. The Mayor of Port Talbot, Alderman Mel John, is seated fifth from the left.

The scene outside the Civic Centre, Port Talbot, on the occasion of the visit of Princess Anne, 29 September 1989. The Civic Centre, which had been brought into use in March 1987, was officially opened by the Princess Royal and the theatre within the building was named in her honour.

Five

Transport and Communication

Captain Oliver Fenton of Twyn-y-Deri, Baglan Road, Port Talbot was one of the earliest motorists in Glamorgan. Here, he is seen at the turn of the century in his first car – an 1899 Stanley steamer (registration number: L36). This car would have been imported from the United States as it was designed by the famous Stanley twins while they were running a photographic dry-plate business in Massachusetts. What looks like a radiator in front is actually a condenser for the steam-engine. These cars were silent, efficient, and simple to drive. However, it took some minutes to raise steam, they had to be filled with water every few hours, and the flues required regular cleaning.

Some early examples of motor-cars (and pedal power!) outside the Abbey Church of St Mary the Virgin, Margam, 1920s.

The railway sidings in front of Margam Terrace in the 1930s. The group standing in front of the 0-6-0 saddle tank locomotive are from left to right: Fred Roddis junior, -?-, -?-, Fred Roddis senior (engine driver).

Fred Roddis and Margaret Roddis posing with their two Vauxhall Cresta taxis in Devonshire Place, late 1960s. The taxi business, consisting of an Alvis and an old Vauxhall, was started by Fred and his father in the late 1940s. The Vauxhall was eventually replaced by a Buick and then a Humber Super Snipe was bought in place of the Alvis. Thereafter, both cars were changed every two years. Margaret Roddis started driving the taxis in 1962 and both she and Fred continued running the business until their retirement in November 1988.

Contrary to popular belief, it was not only post-Second World War that Station Road had traffic problems due to the infamous R & SBR (Rhondda & Swansea Bay Railway) line level-crossing gates. The view on this early postcard from c. 1925 shows that traffic has always been something of a problem in Port Talbot. This photograph also gives a wealth of information in enabling a number of business premises to be identified from their sun blinds.

A typical scene in Station Road, looking east, 1959, showing the build-up of traffic due to the closing of the level-crossing gates. The suffering was to continue for another five years until 1964 when, as a result of the 'Beeching Axe', traffic ceased on the R&SB Railway. The station at Aberavon and the level-crossing gates were subsequently demolished the same year. However, full relief for through traffic did not come until 1971, when the inner ring-road, Heilbronn Way, was opened.

Not all traffic hold-ups, however, were caused by the level-crossing, as demonstrated in this 1959 photograph. A massive Wynn's tractor pulls an even bigger load through the town leaving very little room for vehicles to pass in the opposite direction and no chance for anything to overtake it.

Terry Vaughan and the author standing alongside their Morris J-type GPO van parked outside the telephone exchange at the Abbey Works general offices, 1958. The two GPO engineers were engaged in extending the telephone-exchange switchboard and, like many hundreds of other suffering fellow travellers, had to endure the Port Talbot traffic problem twice every day for what seemed to be an eternity.

When the Abbey Works first opened, everyone seemed to travel to and from work by public transport: either on the train, which stopped at the specially-built works halt, or on the buses. There were a number of large bus parks located strategically throughout the works: on Central Road, for example, as shown in this 1952 photograph (*left*). From these locations, employees could be transported to and from any part of the plant by the Steel Company of Wales's own fleet of buses, or 'brakes' as they were called. There were 16 of these brakes in service in 1952 (*right*).

The construction of the M4 motorway well underway at Groes in 1975. This panoramic view shows that the 'Round Chapel' had already been dismantled and moved for re-erection on its new site in Tollgate Gardens. The remainder of the village had been flattened and shortly after this photograph was taken, the old school in the foreground was razed to the ground. The garage of Margam Abbey Motors can be seen in the distance awaiting the same fate.

The elevated section of the M4 motorway snaking its way above the houses of Port Talbot and Aberavon, October 1991.

Antiquary, one of the 0-4-0 broad-gauge locomotives operated by the GWR which provided all the engines and rolling stock for the South Wales Railway opened in 1850.

Urmston, an 0-6-0 saddle tank used during the construction of the Port Talbot Dock and Railway Yards, 1890–1910 (from the West Glamorgan Archive Service collection, ref: D/D Z 276).

Saddle-tank steam-locomotive (No 401), one of a special class delivered to the Steel Company of Wales's Margam Works engine sheds in 1951, was used in the heaviest service with conspicuous success. These were among the most powerful steam-locomotives in use throughout the plant and had an 0-6-0 wheel arrangement. However, in September 1957, steam gave way to diesel. No 401 and all the other steam-engines in the works were retired and a new breed of diesel-powered locomotives took their place.

An iron-ore train waiting for the clear signal on the sidings at Abbey Works, 1987. These trains run a regular shuttle service carrying iron ore from the deep-water-harbour stockyards at Port Talbot to British Steel's Llanwern Works. This train is being hauled by British Rail main-line diesel locomotives *Castell Ogwr/Ogwr Castle* (No 56304), in front, and *Richard Trevithick* (No 56037) in support.

Port Talbot main-line station, *c.* 1920.

Port Talbot station does not seem to have changed much in nearly eighty years, but the mode of rail travel certainly has. In this photograph taken in 1989, an Inter City HS 125 express pauses on its journey from Paddington to Swansea. Since their introduction in the late 1970s, these expresses have significantly reduced journey times between South Wales and London.

The Queen and the Duke of Edinburgh arriving at Port Talbot station during their visit to open the new basic-oxygen-steel-making plant at the Abbey Works and the new deep-water tidal harbour, 12 May 1970.

Another important arrival at Port Talbot station – Father Christmas – being welcomed by the Mayor of Port Talbot, Cllr Mel John, and Cllr Lance Heycock in 1971.

Six

Religion

The remains of the chapter-house at Margam Abbey, 1887. Although several polygonal chapter-houses still remain intact (for example, at Westminster Abbey, Wells, and Lincoln), the magnificent twelve-sided construction at Margam was almost unique in Cistercian architecture. Another example is known to have existed at Abbey Dore, but very little of this now remains standing. The Margam Abbey chapter-house was probably built about 1200. As simplicity was the keynote of the Cistercian order, it is a plain but elegant structure. Designed to be polygonal on the outside, the internal walls are circular with a diameter of 15.24m (50ft). It is a sad reflection on the Mansel family who acquired the Abbey after the dissolution of the monasteries, that they allowed the building to fall into decay and eventual ruin. An engraving made in 1780 shows that the chapter-house had a beautiful groined roof supported by a clustered central column. Prior to 1760, the lead had been stripped from the roof to repair another building on the Margam estate. By 1787, the central column was sadly out of true and the vaulting was open in several places. So much so that by 1793 two windows and much of the central pillar had fallen down.

A civic service was held in the Abbey Church of St Mary the Virgin on 8 June 1997 to commemorate the 850th anniversary of the founding of Margam Abbey in 1147. From left to right, front row: Luke Mainwaring (Port Talbot Sea Cadets), Robert C. Hastie (Lord Lieutenant of West Glamorgan), Mrs Hastie, Revd Derek Belcher (vicar of Margam), Rt Revd Roy T. Davies (Bishop of Llandaff), Cllr Mel John and Barbara John (Mayor and Mayoress of Neath Port Talbot County Borough Council), Anthony Radcliffe (people's warden), Henri Griffiths, (vicar's warden), Malcolm Wills (head verger). The bishop's chaplain, James Thomas and David Lloyd-Jones, are standing behind the two church-wardens. Margam Abbey was the third great religious house to be built in Glamorgan by the Norman conquerors, its founder being Robert, earl of Gloucester. He was the eldest of King Henry I's natural sons and, prior to his death in 1147, he offered the land on which the Abbey was to be built to Bernard, abbot of Clairvaux, south-east of Paris.

Also to commemorate the 850th anniversary of the founding of Margam Abbey, the West Glamorgan Archive Service, under the direction of Susan Beckley, county archivist, published a limited facsimile edition of Walter de Gray Birch's famous book of 1897, the *History of Margam Abbey*. Miss Beckley, fourth from the left in the photograph, is seen here at the book launch in Margam Abbey on 8 June 1997. From left to right: Canon David Walker (who wrote a short essay to enhance the facsimile edition), Rt Revd Roy T. Davies (Lord Bishop of Llandaff), Cllr Mel John and Barbara John (Mayor and Mayoress of Neath Port Talbot County Borough Council).

The interior of the Abbey Church of St Mary the Virgin, Margam, *c*. 1910.

The alabaster tombs and effigies of the Mansel Talbots. Following the dissolution of the monasteries by Henry VIII, Sir Rice Mansel of Gower acquired the lease of a fair-sized portion of Margam Abbey on the day after the monks had been evicted in 1537. By October 1540, he had purchased this property which included the Abbey church and bell-tower, and a large part of the Margam estate, for £938 6s 8*d*. Thereafter, he continued to buy up remaining parcels of the Abbey's once-extensive estates. The last Lord Mansel died in 1750 and the Margam estates passed to the Talbots of Lacock.

An unusual view of the south side of the Abbey Church of St Mary the Virgin, *c*. 1912.

The clergyman sitting centrally with the choir, outside the west side of the Abbey Church of St Mary the Virgin, is almost certainly Revd John Bangor Davies, curate-in-charge of St Theodore's Church, Kenfig Hill (1883–1904) and vicar of St James's Church, Pyle (from 1904 until his death in 1915, aged 72).

Some of the staff of the Abbot's Kitchen at Margam Abbey, 1997. From left to right: Revd Derek G. Belcher (vicar of the Abbey Church of St Mary the Virgin), Mollie Kelleher (cellarer), Sharon Belcher (restaurant and bar manager), Gill Davison (parish secretary and catering manager). Even though there has always been catering at Margam, it was run in the past on a seasonal basis. The Abbot's Kitchen, as we know it today, was brought into being when Revd Belcher was appointed to the parish in 1987. With the professionalism that he brought with him, the Abbot's Kitchen took on a new dynamism and now opens six days a week including Sundays.

An unusual view of the remains of the fifteenth-century Capel Mair (also called Hen Eglwys or Cryke Chapel) taken from Mynydd y Castell, 1994. This roofless ruin is known locally as 'Capel y Papishod' (a name derived from the Welsh for papists). It is thought to have been built before 1470, probably to serve the needs of local farmers and peasantry who were not allowed to worship within the Abbey itself. The chapel was roughly built with local sandstone, but enhanced with beautiful windows at each end. The east window bears the remains of tracery of the Perpendicular style suggesting a fifteenth-century date, while the west window appears to be of even earlier origin.

A Roman Catholic mass being held in Capel Mair, Margam, 1993.

The ruins of the old church at Baglan. It was around 1,440 years ago that St Baglan is said to have founded the first church on this site. He was a *peregrini* or wandering missionary who travelled between Wales and Brittany. Legend has it that he had been told to go to a place where he would find a tree that bore three sorts of fruit and erect a church for himself there. Led by a staff given to him by St Illtud, he had arrived in Baglan, but ignored this advice and made several attempts to build a church on the low-lying moors. However, what building he erected in the day was taken away in the night. Finally, he found a tree that had a litter of pigs at its roots, a hive of bees in its trunk, and a crow's nest at the top. He interpreted this as being the tree with three fruits and built his church on the hill which overlooks the present church of St Catherine. The old church built in the twelfth century is derelict now, crazily crowning the hill and tilted slightly off the vertical. It was last used for services in 1882.

BAGLAN, ABERAVON.   W.413.

St Catherine's Church, Baglan, pre-Second World War, before extensive building of houses on the old Baglan Hall estate began. The church cost over £17,000 to build and was the gift of Mr Griffith and Madelina Georgina Llewellyn of Baglan Hall. Mrs Llewellyn laid the foundation stone on 26 June 1875 and the church was consecrated by Dr Ollivant, bishop of Llandaff, on 7 March 1882. According to local tradition, Mr Griffith Llewellyn insisted that it should take seven years to build and that all stone dressing and carpentry be done outside the church boundary wall so that 'neither hammer nor axe, nor any tool of iron, be heard in the house while it is in the building'.

The vicar of Baglan, Revd David Lewis, pointing out the intricacies of the Brancuf stone. This stone, which is of considerable archaeological significance, is set in the vestry wall of St Catherine's Church and was used as a coping stone in the old churchyard. Measuring $27\frac{1}{2}$ in x 16in), the stone bears a carved Latin wheel cross in low relief. The decoration shows Irish influence suggesting that the old church is on the site of a much earlier Celtic building.

The peal of six bells of St Catherine's Church, Baglan, was dedicated on 29 January 1900. The photograph shows the original tenor and treble bells that were brought down to be recast to be in tune with the four new bells. The two boys are Jack and Godfrey Llewellyn, the latter sitting on the bell that bears his name.

A clean-up of the graveyard of St Mary's Church, Aberavon, by volunteers in 1976. St Mary's, the parish church of Aberavon, was largely rebuilt in 1859 from the fabric of a 14th-century building.

The new cross erected near the porch of St Mary's Church, Aberavon, in the early 1970s to mark the grave of Richard Lewis (Dic Penderyn). The inscription on the memorial reads: 'TO THE MEMORY OF RICHARD LEWIS EXECUTED AT CARDIFF FOR THE PART HE PLAYED DURING THE INDUSTRIAL RIOTS IN MERTHYR TYDFIL IN JUNE 1831. BURIED ON 14TH AUGUST 1831 AGED 23 YEARS'. Wales's first working-class martyr, Lewis was a young miner who was charged with wounding a soldier during the Merthyr riots of 1831. Despite widespread conviction of his innocence and concerted petitioning against the sentence, he was executed. A large crowd accompanied his body from Cardiff to St Mary's Church in Aberavon, his birthplace.

Water-colour exhibition by A. Leslie Evans in the St Mary's Church Centre, Aberavon, 1981. Mr Evans is seen presenting the Mayor of Port Talbot, Cllr Val Kingdom, with a water-colour of the 'Round Chapel' at Groes. Also in the picture are Mrs V. Evans, Revd G. Hopkins (vicar of St Mary's Church and rural dean), with J.T. Jones in the background.

Archbishop Mostyn of Cardiff, with senior members of the parish, after laying the foundation stone for the new St Joseph's Church, Aberavon, on 11 September 1930. Also in the photograph are Canon Kelly, Father Gavin, W. Greenway, David Murphy, James O'Brien JP, John O'Donovan, Timothy and Edward Madden, Joseph Kenure, Gustav Wehrle, and Dan McCarthy.

Officers and council of St Joseph's (Aberavon) Catholic Young Men's Society, 1928–29. From left to right, back row: Brothers P. Lahive, D. Bright, J. Lahive, T. Wilkins, M. Lahive; middle row: Brothers J. Mahoney, D. John, J. Downey, J. Waters, J. Madden, J.L. O'Brien; seated: J.W. Dowling (chief warden), J. Moran (vice-president), the Very Revd Phillip Canon Kelly (spiritual director), J. O'Donovan (president of St Joseph's Catholic Young Men's Society and president of CYMS of Great Britain), Revd P. Gavin, W. Greenway (hon treasurer) and E.G. Madden (hon secretary).

The choir, clergy, rural deans of the diocese, and the bishop of Llandaff with his chaplain, processing into the newly-built St Theodore's Church, Port Talbot, for the opening and dedication ceremony held on Thursday, 5 August 1897. The church was built by Emily Talbot of Margam House in memory of her brother Theodore and sister Olivia. The consecration service was conducted by the bishop, and the church was dedicated to St Theodore of Tarus.

This group photograph was taken on the occasion of the 50th anniversary of St Theodore's Church in 1947. From left to right, standing: Frank Seaton (organist), W. George (church-warden), Major Llewellyn David (church-warden); seated: Revd Glyn Bowen (assistant priest, later to become vicar), Revd Eric Roberts (vicar, later to become bishop of St Davids), and Revd Trevor Price (assistant priest).

The vicar, Revd Colin Amos, and Beryl George outside St Theodore's Church with the two booklets published to mark the centenary of the church, 5 August 1997. Miss George, a life-long worshipper in the church, has produced a very comprehensive history and guide to St Theodore's Church. Elected to the parochial church council in 1974 and church treasurer since 1986, Miss George has also been a Sunday school teacher (1944-84), PCC secretary (1978-89) and people's church-warden (1978-86).

Bishop Glyn Symonds, with choir in attendance, at the foundation-stone-laying ceremony for St David's Church, 16 October 1958. The stone was laid by W.F. Cartwright DL, JP, general manager (Steel Division) at the Steel Company of Wales Ltd.

St David's Church fête, 1976, with comedian Ryan Davies, centre, and Revd Glyn Bowen, vicar, on his left.

The re-opening of Beulah Chapel (the 'Round Chapel') on its new site in Tollgate Gardens, Margam, 22 April 1976. The chapel, originally built in 1838, had been dismantled brick by brick to make way for the M4 motorway which passed right through the now demolished village of Groes. It has considerable architectural interest with its mullioned windows and octagonal shape. Local folklore has it that it was built that way so that there would be no corners in which the Devil could hide.

The Aberavon Salvation Army Band, c. 1910.

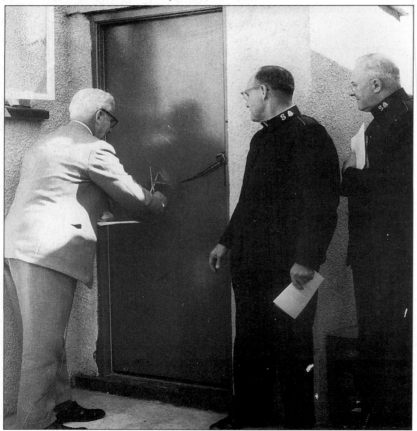

David J. Young, secretary of the Steel Company of Wales Ltd, opening the Salvation Army Hall, Port Talbot, in 1963.

The Zion Chapel Whitsun march passing Locke's, the saddler's shop in High Street, Aberavon, *c*. 1900. The procession was led by the banner-bearers and hymns were sung throughout the march.

Opening of the St Michael's and All Saints' Church fête, Cwmavon, 1930s. From left to right:
-?-, Mrs W.D. McNeil, Charles Jenkins, Revd John Washington Jones, Oliver Carlill, the earl of
Jersey, Bishop Timothy Rees, Mrs Davies (London Row, seated), John Lewis, Revd Isaac D.
Rosser, Superintendent Rees Davies, Miss Crawshay Williams, Rees John (newsagent), W.G.
McNeil (vicar's warden), Mr Beynon.

Going, going, gone! The final
moments of All Saints'
Church before the spire was
demolished with explosives in
1980. Built in 1855 on land
that had been attached to
Ynys Afan (a monastic grange
belonging to Margam Abbey),
the church was a chapel of
ease to St Michael's Church,
Cwmavon.

Seven

Education

The infants' class of Aberavon Council (the Mountain) School, c. 1908. Note how serious the children are looking; there is not a smile amongst the lot of them. This appears to be a prerequisite of all school-group photographs taken during this period! The manner of dress is also interesting with the majority of the girls wearing white smocks and the boys with either white-lace or stiff, starched collars.

Standards V and VI at Eastern Boys School, 1911–12. How many of us can still remember attending a classroom like this and sitting in the fixed desks with their hinged lids, white ink-wells on the top and a groove for pens and pencils?

The girls of class I at Aberavon Council (the Mountain) School, *c.* 1910.

Girls at Aberavon Council School, *c*. 1908.

The school at Groes village, Margam, *c*. 1910. This was built in 1866 at a cost to the Margam estate of £667 17s. Thomas F. Howell was appointed as the first headmaster on a salary of £52 10s. He was later assisted by his wife Lucy, and Louisa Eley, the daughter of C.R.M. Talbot's coachman. Later head teachers of Groes School were Phoebe O'Connor (1879–84), A. Derrick (1884–91), W.R. Mills (1891–97), A. Morris (1897–1905), and W.A. Brown (1905–31). After serving the community for nearly 110 years, the school, along with the village of Groes, was demolished in 1975 to make way for the extension of the M4 motorway (*see also page 52*).

Members of the Kenfig Society outside what was the Margam Church School, 1994. Built in the late eighteenth century, the school was closed in 1866 and local children transferred to the newly-built school in Groes village. The building now houses the Margam Stones Museum administered by CADW.

Teachers and children of Groes School, Margam, in the 1920s.

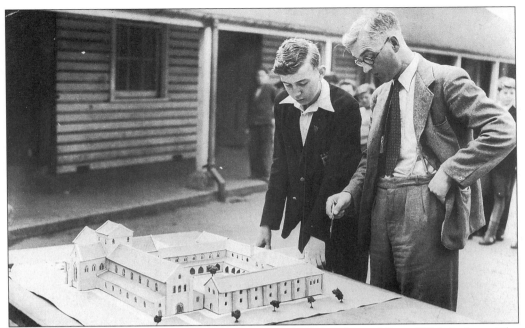

A. Leslie Evans inspecting a scale-model of Margam Abbey with pupil Peter Whittingham. The model had been made by pupils of Park (Central) School, 1958.

Staff of the Central Boys School, Port Talbot, January 1948. From left to right: A. Leslie Evans, D.H. Thomas, H. Davies, P. Rees, Elwyn Williams, George Rees, W. Harries, F. Bish, S. Vaughan (headmaster), J. Williams.

St Joseph's Church Green Stars schoolboy rugby team, Aberavon, late 1880s. This is the earliest photograph in existence of the Green Stars. The man standing on the left of the picture is H. Carrol.

Port Talbot Secondary Grammar School rugby team, 1943. From left to right, back row: C. Reynolds (headmaster), Owain Davies, Roy Vincent, Eric Lambourne, Iestyn Francis, Llew Thomas, Graham Bish, Mr ? Phillips; middle row: Howard Joseph, Ken Arnold, Brinley Jenkins, Bryn Phillips (captain), Richard Jenkins, Ken Williams, Gerald Lewis; front row: Alun Edwards, Ralph Ackery, Aubrey Hibbs, Gerwyn Davies. The young Richard Jenkins in the middle row was later to become famous as the actor and film star Richard Burton. During his school rugby career, he had three schoolboy international rugby trials. It was after Richard had been reinstated (after having left to work in the local Co-op) at Port Talbot Secondary Grammar School in 1942 that he received the training and encouragement of Phil Burton, the English teacher at the school whose surname he took as his stage-name.

Eight
Organisations

Gwyneth Mair Jenkins of Waun-Bant Road, Kenfig Hill, on duty as a nursing cadet with the St John Ambulance Brigade at the 1932 National Eisteddfod held in Port Talbot.

A police sergeant of the Glamorgan Constabulary in his full winter-issue uniform, outside the main gates of the Margam estate, *c.* 1910.

Members of the Margam District Council Fire Brigade on parade in full-dress uniform with their fire-fighting appliance, *c.* 1910. The officer-in-charge, Captain Tom Hughes, is standing third from the left by the wheel.

Members of the Margam Urban District Council, 1905. This council was formed in 1894 and remained in force until 1921 when it was amalgamated with Aberavon Borough to form the new Port Talbot Borough. The bearded man in the front row is D.R. David with Major Thomas Gray (the historian) sitting behind the dog on his left. Standing in the centre of the second row is Sydney H. Byass who was the last mayor of Aberavon and the first of Port Talbot.

Aberavon General Hospital fête in 1924 when the guest of honour was local MP, and then Labour's first-ever prime minister, Ramsay MacDonald. Whenever he had the occasion to visit his constituency at this time, MacDonald was welcomed with huge rallies.

The Cwmavon Philharmonic Glee Society, 1929–37, with conductor Rowland Hill seated in the centre of the front row. There has always been a strong tradition of choral singing in South Wales, especially so in this area.

The 'Israel Relieved' scene from the Cwmavon Choral Society's presentation of Mendelssohn's *Elijah*. Performances were given at the Copper Miners Hall, Cwmavon, from 21 to 26 April 1947. The producer and director was Eddie Thomas, and Rowland Hill conducted a philharmonic orchestra led by Morgan Lloyd. The accompanists were Mrs Rowland Hill and Oswald Phillips. The cast consisted of George Thomas in the title role of Elijah, Tom Thomas as Obadiah, Jennet Mainwaring as the widow, Joan Rees as the chief angel, Leonard Stephens as the king, Madam Arianwen Lind as the queen, Gwenfil Harris as the youth, and Freda Williams as the solo dancer.

Two scenes from performances given by the Port Talbot and Aberavon Amateur Operatic Society. *Left*: Lyn and Beatrice Howell in the 1929 production of *Havana* in the New Theatre, Port Talbot. *Right*: Bert Farcott as Emile La Flamme in the 1933 production of *Rose Marie*.

The cast of the Port Talbot and Aberavon Amateur Operatic Society's 1934 production of *Rio Rita*.

The Steel Company of Wales Male Voice Choir, with musical director Rowland Hill, on stage at the Odeon Theatre, Port Talbot, Sunday, 14 November 1948. The soloist shown in the photograph was the tenor Luigi Infantino of La Scala opera-house, Milan. His co-artiste was soprano Sheila de Haan, only 21 years old at the time of the concert. The accompanists were Norman John and Joan Inglesant while the guest accompanist was Stewart Nash. This was the fourth annual international celebrity concert; the first was given in 1937 with the proceeds of the concert going to the Manor House Hospital at Golders Green, London.

Mr and Mrs Rowland Hill, both of whom played important roles as musical director and accompanist, respectively, for the Cwmavon Philharmonic Glee Society, the Cwmavon Choral Society, the Port Talbot and Aberavon Amateur Operatic Society, and the Steel Company of Wales Male Voice Choir.

The Steel Company of Wales Male Voice Choir under the musical direction of Rowland Hill, photographed prior to their performance at the fifth international celebrity concert, 1949. The latter was again held in the Odeon Cinema, Port Talbot, with guest artistes Luigi Infantino (tenor) and Sylvia Fisher (soprano). The guest accompanist was Stewart Nash.

Gilbert and Sullivan's comic opera *The Pirates of Penzance* presented at the New Hall, Aberavon, April 1948. This was the first stage performance given by the newly formed Afan and District Amateur Operatic Society after their inauguration in 1947. Fifty years on, the now retitled Port Talbot and District Amateur Operatic Society, is still giving first-class performances to appreciative audiences. To celebrate the 50th anniversary, a gala evening was given in the Princess Royal Theatre, Port Talbot, on 16 and 17 October 1996. The programme on this special occasion was made up of selections taken from many of the operas and musicals performed by the society over the past 50 years.

The cast of *Iolanthe*, another Gilbert and Sullivan classic, presented by the Afan & District Amateur Operatic Society in the New Hall, Port Talbot, 24–29 March 1952. Aurelia Vowles John (a founder member and the first musical director of the society) is seated centre of the second row between J. Norman John (another past musical director and honorary patron of the society), on her right, and Len Dix (the guest producer), on her left.

The Afan & District Amateur Operatic Society has also presented a fine selection of musicals over the years. *Calamity Jane* was performed at the comprehensive school, Sandfields estate in 1968. The title role of Calamity Jane, the hard-bitten, gun-totin' heroine, who tries to behave like a man, but can't help loving like a woman (!) was played on this occasion by buck-skin-dressed Mavis Richards, centre.

The cast of the first performance of *Behold the Man* by the Port Talbot Passion Play Association, outside the Abbey Church of St Mary the Virgin, Margam, 1978. *Behold the Man* was written by a local author, the late Leo Arthurs. This spectacular portrayal of the greatest story ever told, is now performed every two years as an open-air event running over two weeks. About 150 people take part in what is a family affair, including parents and children, with many teenagers in the cast.

Passion play being performed on the steps of Bethany Chapel, Port Talbot, in the 1980s.

Members of the British Legion marching at the VE-Day 50th-anniversary parade, Port Talbot, 1995.

Presentation on behalf of the Port Talbot Historical Society to A. Leslie Evans in the St Mary's Church Centre, Aberavon, 1996. The picture shows Mr Evans receiving a wristlet-watch from the president of the society, Dr Prys Morgan, and an illuminated scroll from Arthur Hughes, chairman and photographic secretary. The scroll was presented on the occasion of Leslie's election as patron of the society and as a token of their appreciation of his dedicated service as vice-chairman and chairman for over 42 years. As well as his work as a local historian, Leslie also had another not-so-well-known talent, that of writing children's stories in one of the local papers.

The Mayor of Port Talbot, Cllr Mel John, presiding over the Port Talbot Onion Show in 1971.

First, second, and third prizes in the rose section of the Cwmavon Garden and Allotment Association's show held on 14 August 1976, were won by Alan Hopkin. He is seen here with his trophy – the rose bowl – and his children Robert (aged 5) and Allison (8), who are admiring his prize exhibits.

A young Joan Poston presenting a bunch of prize winning chrysanthemums to Mrs Howe at one of the annual shows of the Port Talbot and District Chrysanthemums Society held in the late 1950s. Among the members of the society in the picture are: Wilf H. Poston (treasurer), Cyril Jenkins (secretary), Percy Penhorwood (chairman).

Wilf H. Poston (centre) being presented with a clock by Mr Penhorwood, chairman of the Port Talbot and District Chrysanthemums Society, for services rendered to the society, 1960. A qualified horticultural judge for 15 years and a founder-member and treasurer of the society, Wilf had also been awarded the National Chrysanthemum Silver Medal. Mrs Irene Poston is on the left.

Nine
Views and Scenery

Flooding outside the Plaza Cinema, Port Talbot, when the river Afan burst its banks in the 1970s.

A view looking up the Afan valley to Cwmavon, *c.* 1910. Note the small hill on the immediate right of the photograph – Craig Avon (*see page 11*).

A general view of Cwmavon, *c.* 1920.

Talbot Street, Port Talbot, *c.* 1900.

The old general post office, Station Road, before it was demolished in 1975 during the construction of Heilbronn Way, the inner ring-road. The building, erected in 1912, not only housed the post office, but was home to the multiple-switchboard manual telephone-exchange, the telegraph office, and the postal sorting-office.

The mill, Efail Fach, Pontrhydyfen, *c.* 1910. A literal translation of the Welsh name 'Pontrhydyfen', means 'the bridge over the ford by the waters'. Indeed, two rivers do merge here at this junction of two valleys.

No 2 Dan-y-bont, Pontrhydyfen, the house where Richard Walter Jenkins was born on 10 November 1925. This was the name that he used for the first seventeen years of his life until he adopted the surname 'Burton' by which he is now better known. Inside the porch, there is a plaque on the wall which marks the fact. Yr Hen Bont, the viaduct which overshadows the house, was built in the late 1820s to carry water and a tramway to the nearby Oakwood iron works. Today, it remains as a ramblers' footpath.

The main lodge and gates to Margam Park, *c.* 1910.

The west lodge to Margam Park, *c.* 1910. This was demolished to make way for the extension to the M4 motorway in 1975.

Donkey and trap in Margam Park, c. 1910.

Morfa Mawr Farm, Morfa Moors, c. 1955. This was built by C.R.M. Talbot as a hunting and shooting lodge in the 1830s, but was used mainly as a farmhouse. Morfa Mawr Farm, sited near to the sea, and the 'Round Chapel' at Groes were designed by the same architect and both incorporate features suggestive of a medieval influence. It was eventually demolished in December 1975 to make way for development of the area by the British Steel Corporation.

Ten

Events

Street party in Vivian Square, Aberavon, held to celebrate the silver jubilee of King George V in 1935. The following appear in the photograph: Liz Howells, Annie Manchip, Mary Jones, Helen McGrath, Eva Perry, Maggie Fleming, Evelyn Peters, Alice Llewellyn, Lil Manchip, Doris Hughes, Mrs Richards, Mrs Peters, Mrs W. Richards, Martha Richards, Mrs Bernard O'Leary, Mrs W. Davies, Mrs Davies senior, Mrs Phillips, Olive Phillips, Ethel Phillips, Maggie Howlet, Irene Potter, Mrs Morris, Iris Williams, Mrs W. Donovan, Nellie Bennet, Maggie Llewellyn, Katie Llewellyn, Mrs M. McGrath, Mrs P. McGrath, Mrs Howlet, Louise Howlet, Janet Jones, Maggie Llewellyn, Kath Richards, Florrie Manchip, Doris Jones, Mary Fleming, Clem Perry, Mrs Bennet, Mary O'Leary, Beryl Aston, Mrs W. Aston, Dai Thomas, and Michael Donovan.

The Cwmavon carnival queen and her attendants, 1976.

A scene from the Royal Navy Club carnival, 1976.

The first Aberavon Round-the-Pier Swim, 1969. This took place in response to an open invitation from the Port Talbot Borough Council for clubs in the area to do something out of the ordinary to mark the occasion of the Investiture of Prince Charles as Prince of Wales that year. The Green Stars Rugby Football Club proposed the idea of holding a land and sea swimming race around the old Aberavon pier. The president of the club, Frank Burke, presented two Prince of Wales Investiture trophies to be competed for in the race: one for the winner of the open event, the other for the first club member to cross the finishing line. An estimated crowd of over 5,000 people watched the race which was such an outstanding success that it has become an annual event ever since. Most of the local swimmers who took part were already competitors in the annual Mumbles to Aberavon Swim.

The start of the 1972 Aberavon Round-the-Pier Swim. The combined land and sea swimming race both starts and finishes at the Green Stars RFC clubhouse with the swim around the old pier forming the central activity. The race was won by student Allan Davies of Channel View, Port Talbot.

Another local water event, the River Avon Raft Race, 1976.

Left: 'South Sea island girls', complete with raffia skirts, providing encouragement for the entrants in the 1976 River Avon Raft Race. *Right*: Ron McConville with local author, Elaine Crowley, who is signing copies of her book *Dreams of Other Days* in his newsagent's and bookshop, Station Road, *c.* 1976.

Sally Burton, with Brook Williams (son of the late Emlyn Williams), on her right, at Richard Burton's memorial service, Pontrhydyfen, Saturday, 11 August 1984. Richard Burton had died in Switzerland on the previous Sunday.

Bill Jenkins and Richard Burton's sisters (from left to right: Hilda, Cis and Cassie) at Richard's memorial service in Pontrhydyfen, 1984. It was his eldest sister Cis, who had brought up and looked after 'Rich' as a child after his mother died in 1927.

An occasion not to be forgotten. The scene outside Bethel Chapel, Pontryhydyfen, for Richard Burton's memorial service on Saturday, 11 August 1984. Over 400 friends had squeezed inside the chapel while outside twice that number listened to the service over the tannoy and joined in the singing of the hymns.

Another local boy cast in the same mould as Richard Burton and destined not only to reach stardom and fame as an actor and film star, but to achieve the honour of knighthood as well. The photograph shows Sir Anthony Hopkins receiving the Freedom of the Borough of Port Talbot from Keri Lewis (chief executive), and the mayor, Cllr Noel Crowley, 1994.

Lord Howe of Aberavon, another native of Aberavon, with his wife Lady Howe, after receiving the Freedom of the Borough of Port Talbot in 1992.

The Mayor of Port Talbot, Cllr Olga Jones, under the watchful eye of the fire officer, lighting the VE-day-50th-anniversary beacon on Aberavon Sands, 1995.

HRH The Princess Anne, talking to the crowds outside the Civic Centre, Port Talbot, after she had performed the opening ceremony of the building on 29 September 1989.

Every dog has his day. The dog-show section of the British Steel Corporation's family day in the early 1970s. From extreme left to right: Ridian Angell, the author, Malvina Morgan, and Neil Angell in front holding Rebel, the shaggy-haired dog that went on to win the 'dog with the waggiest tail' competition.

Eleven

War Years

Flintlock pistol and powder horn used by David Rees (1847–1944) during his service under the command of the Hon C.R.M. Talbot MP in the old Margam Volunteer Rifle Corps. (The unit was eventually to become part of the 1st Administration Battalion, Glamorgan Rifle Corps, with two companies.) The medal was presented for long service in the unit. David, a member of the famous Margam Bando Boys, had the honour to be on parade when the Prince and Princess of Wales (afterwards King Edward VII and Queen Alexandra) visited Margam Castle on 17 October 1881.

Members of the Kenfig Society in what might have been a look-out post on top of Craig y Lodge, above Margam Castle, during their annual walk in 1994. The Margam Volunteer Rifles were formed in 1859 under the threat of a possible French invasion and this post was possibly built at the same time.

The remains of what could be either a Second-World-War search-light station or coastal gun battery, 1994. The site is located inside the Iron Age camp on the top of Mynydd y Castell. Further to the west, an early type of radar station was built at the beginning of the Second World War on the scarp of Mynydd Margam to cover Swansea Bay (*see page 10*). After the blitz on Swansea, coastal defence was increased and four 3.7-inch anti-aircraft guns together with a radar station were located at Morfa Mawr Farm. The RAF also had a practice firing-range in a field adjacent to this farm. A target was fixed on a small trolley that travelled from side to side on a curved course along a narrow-gauge railway.

Following the fall of France in 1940, Local Volunteer Defence units were formed, later to be renamed as the Home Guard. The photograph shows members of the 20th Battalion, Glamorgan Home Guard, *c.* 1943.

Left: the late Rennie Davies, chairman of the Kenfig Society, on top of the Second-World-War pill-box on Kenfig dunes, April 1993. *Right*: the remains of another Second-World-War relic, an RAF quadrant tower at Morfa, being examined by Mick Cliff, manager of information services at British Steel's Port Talbot Works, 1997. It has slipped down from the top of the sand dune on which it was originally positioned, but being of solid concrete construction – a credit to its wartime designers and builders – it is still in one piece. However, because of the crazy angle at which it has come to rest, standing upright on the sloping floor gives one an eerie sensation of vertigo and imbalance as if the tower was still on the move! The towers were erected early in the war to overlook the target area of the bombing range that extended from Morfa to Sker Point and enable the accuracy of bombing exercises to be determined.

A photograph taken by Gerard Lahive in 1991 of all that remains of a Second-World-War tank buried deep in the sand on Morfa Beach. Following enquiries made by Ray Cottrell of the *Glamorgan Gazette*, the Tank Museum at Bovington Camp in Dorset, confirmed that the tank was a Centaur (or possibly a Cromwell depending on the size of its engine). It is thought that the tank was used for pre-D-day landing and sticking trials as similar blue clay exists on both the Normandy and Morfa beaches. Bill Bamsey can remember the tank still had its turret when as boys, they used to play in it. On one occasion, his brother John got stuck inside the turret with the top down and the tide coming in. They had to call the RAF lads from the quadrant tower to help release John.

Photograph of an actual Centaur tank provided by the Tank Museum, Bovington Camp, Dorset. This was not the only vehicle that left it track marks during the Second World War on Morfa sands. The propaganda film *Nine Men*, 'set' in the Libyan desert, was made on location at Morfa in 1943 by Ealing Studios. Men of the South Wales Borderers and London Irish Rifles were enrolled as extras to play soldiers on both sides. In the final scene, a company of these men supported by two Mk VI Crusader tanks, relieved the nine men who had been under attack from the 'Italians'.

Twelve

Sport

The badge of the Margam Volunteers found by Gerard Lahive in 1992. C.R.M. Talbot formed the Volunteers in May 1859 with most of the men coming from the Margam Bando Boys team, of which he was captain. Hence, the badge is made up of two bando sticks supporting the Volunteers' motto 'MARGAM DROS BYTH' surmounted by a crown. Bando was the most popular sport in the area until the 1870s when it declined in favour of rugby football. It was a strenuous pastime similar to Irish hurling and required a large playing area. Games were held on Kenfig sands with the pitch extending a distance of two miles, from the one goal situated at the mouth of the river Kenfig to the other at Sker Rocks. Matches between rival teams were fast and furious and often lasted for up to four hours. There appeared to be no definite rules other than to win you had to hit a small leather-bound ball with your curved bando stick over your opponents' goal line. In its heyday, there was great support for the game with many thousands turning out to watch matches.

This is the oldest photograph in existence of an Aberavon Rugby Football Club team. It was taken in August 1888 and shows from left to right, back row: Mr Buller (or Butler), Tom Jones, Bill Wilkins, Tom Shaw Roberts, -?-, Jack Harris, Dick Thomas, -?-; second row: Bill Clements, Sam Lewis, Ivor Griffiths (captain), Billie Grace, Joe Hopkins, and George Bowen; front row: Rees Hopkins and Jonathan Peters. The club was initially formed in 1876; it disbanded for a time in the 1880s, but was reformed in 1887 and has flourished ever since. The captain in this photograph, Ivor Griffiths, led the side for seven years.

The re-opening of the Aberavon RFC's Central Athletic Ground, Port Talbot, on 3 December 1921, by Sidney H. Byass, president of the club. During the First World War the pitch had been turned into allotments. With the club's ground situated in Port Talbot all games could be said to be played away! An earlier venue for a ground was at Port Talbot Docks where, between 1878 and the mid-1880s, games were played on a pitch known as Wharf Field.

The Aberavon XV that played against Neath to celebrate the re-opening of the Central Athletic Ground, Port Talbot, on 3 December 1921. From left to right, back row: W.J. Ould, J. Jeremy, G. Bamsey; second row, standing: H. Leyshon, O. Harris, G. Mears, J.H. Davies, W.J. 'Noisy' Thomas, Bob Randell, D. Hunt Davies, Tom Ponsford, G. Reed, H.M. Fuller (referee, Ammanford); front row, seated: Dai Williams, T. Collins, Sydney H. Byass (president, Aberavon RFC), Jim Jones (captain), Horace Lyne (president, Welsh Rugby Union), C.F. Rowlands, T. Parker, Johnnie Ring; cross-legged: Willie Jones, W.J. Hopkins.

Following the end of the Second World War, the 'Kiwis', a touring team made up of New Zealand Army soldiers who had fought in Italy, visited Aberavon in 1946. This photograph is of the Aberavon team that turned out to play the visitors in front of a crowd of 19,000 – reputed to be the largest-ever attendance for a game at the Athletic Club Ground.

Raising funds for Aberavon RFC in 1971. From left to right: Cllr Mel John (the Mayor of Port Talbot), Lord Heycock, Bryn Thomas.

Looking to the future. Aberavon Under-11s rugby team at the Athletic Club Ground during the 1995–96 season.

St Joseph's Green Stars Rugby Football Club, 1904–05. From left to right, back row: P. McCarthy, M. McCarthy, J. Ellis, H. Hambury, C. Cockran, T. Callaghan, J. Bennett, M. Doyle, M. Sweeny, R. Lyons, F. Donovan (treasurer), M. Brien; second row: H. Carrol (secretary), J. Donovan, E. John, J. Brien (captain), Revd Moore, D. McCarthy, P. Walters, M. Grace; front row: R. Payne, Percy May, J. Cockran.

St Joseph's Catholic Young Men's Society Ex-Schoolboy RFC, Aberavon, winners of the Port Talbot Ex-Schoolboys' League Cup, 1928–29. From left to right, front row: T. McNulty, W. McNulty (with cup), W. Davies; second row, seated: D. Madden, M.O. O'Callaghan (vice-captain), G. Wehrle (chairman), W. Welsh (captain), Revd Gavin, D. O'Callaghan, S. Griffiths; third row, standing: M. Lahive, E.B. Madden (hon secretary), J. Burgess, J. McCarthy, M. McCarthy, E. Mahoney, J. Tobin, T. Madden (committee), J. O'Brien (committee); back row: T. Wilkins (trainer), T. Griffiths, P. Breen, S. Brisland, W. Ryan, M. McCarthy, W. Donovan.

Taibach Rugby Football Club players receiving presentations in July 1976 for their performances during the 1975–76 season. From left to right: Henry Mair (player of the year), Philip Berni (most improved player), Julian Williams (youth player of the year).

Richard Burton and his wife Susan (*née* Hunt) during their visit to the Pontrhydyfen RFC clubhouse in 1976. Standing at the back are Richard's brothers Graham Jenkins (left) and David Jenkins (behind Susan).

Port Talbot Association Football Club in the 1920s.

PORT TALBOT & DISTRICT LEAGUE SHIELD WINNERS 1938-1939.

Baglan Church Association Football Club, Port Talbot & District League Shield winners, 1938–39.

Margam cricket team on a pitch in front of Margam Castle, 1911. The team was mainly formed of estate employees and, at this time, the captain was R. Milner, the head gardener. From research carried out by local historian, the late Leslie Evans, it would appear that the club is 125 years old with 1872 being the year of foundation. The start was made largely due to the sponsorship of Theodore Talbot. A keen player himself and a student of the game, he influenced several good players to form a club in the Margam area. Among these was Dr John Hopkin Davies, a fine cricketer, whose practice was based in Taibach.

Margam Cricket Club, winners of the *Evening Post* Knock-out Challenge Cup, 1937. The team is seen above with the captain and Mrs A.M. Fletcher Talbot. The club joined the South Wales Cricket Association (5th Division) in 1986 after being in the Morgannwg League from the 1960s. 1997 saw Margam Cricket Club (now in the 2nd Division) play against Glamorgan and an Old English XI in July as part of the celebrations for what they thought was their centenary year. Nevertheless, 125 years of cricket is still a worthwhile event to celebrate.

The Llewellyn cricket team, Aberavon, early 1950s. From left to right, front row: Gwyn Williams, John Gibbon (fast bowler), Don Harfield, Ben Phelps with team mascot Derek White, Allan Philips, John Hobbs, Viv Davies; back row: Mr White, -?-, -?-, Ron Hawkins, Ernest Griffiths (fast bowler and the only pre-war player to be in the new team), 'Boyo' Davies, Billy Phelps, -?-, -?-, Harry Davies. The Llewellyn cricket team was reformed after the Second World War, but could not find opponents and so, initially, had to play against old boys of the team.

The Steel Company of Wales cricket team, winners of the South Wales Cricket Association (Division 2) Cup, 1961. From left to right, back row: Colin Davies, Cliff Jones, Ken Hopkins, J.N. Toon (scorer), Bill Richards (chairman), John Williams, Val Antolin, Ray Woodward; front row: Trevor Davies, Norman Hooper, Ira Llewellyn, John Reed (captain), Roy Idell, Dave Lewis, Alcwyn Symons. The team had been formed pre-war in the days of the old Baldwin Steelworks. It joined the league as the Steel Company of Wales Cricket Club in 1957.

Members of the St Theodore's Church Sports Club in front of the old Vicarage, c. 1921. The tennis section went on to become the nucleus of the Port Talbot Tennis Club.

Members of the Steel Company of Wales Tennis Club during the 1960s. Included in the photograph are Jack Lewis, Susie Preece, Kathleen Pollard (all seated), W. Emrys Griffiths, Binne McNeil, Alan Waite, Betty Griffiths, Kitty Fancott (all standing).

The Mayor of Port Talbot, Cllr Mel John, showing his smooth action at Ynys Bowls, 1971.

Boxing was very popular during the early part of the century. This photograph, which includes Willy Sheehy, second from the left, shows a group of boxers in Aberavon.

Some local boxers during the First World War. Three men from Taibach appear in the picture: Jimmy Jenkins (standing extreme left in the back row), Charlie Lucas (standing centre), and Billy Beynon (seated on the left). Billy achieved fame by winning the bantamweight championship of Great Britain in 1913.

The grave of Billy Beynon, bantamweight champion of Great Britain (1913) in the Goytre Cemetery. Note the pair of boxing gloves on either side of the memorial stone.

Twelve

Leisure and
Entertainment

A party of ladies picnicking by the old pier at Aberavon, *c.* 1914.

Beach Road, Aberavon, *c*. 1920.

Aberavon Beach, *c*. 1910, with the crowds taking in the sea-air with a leisurely stroll along the pier and promenade.

Sunday school teachers from St Theodore's Church, Port Talbot, enjoying a day out at Margam Abbey, in the 1930s. From left to right, front row: Harry Daniels, -?-, John Morgan; second row: Amy Daniels, Violet Denner, Miss Matthews, Peggy Matthews. The group are posing by the ruins of the chapter-house in front of the 'Great Wheel Cross' or Cross of Cynfelyn. Both sides of the cross and all four faces of the base are covered with elaborate decorations in low relief. The original stone, which has been dated to the late ninth or early tenth century, is now in the Margam Stones Museum.

The Rees family of Margam entertaining their relatives, the Waite family of Kenfig Hill, to a leisurely day out at the orangery in Margam Park in 1927.

A Guest Keen day trip to Oxford and the river, possibly in the last years before the outbreak of the Second World War. Amongst the crowd on board the river pleasure-craft the following individuals have been identified: Hilda Williams, Doug Collins, Megan Williams, Dorothy Richards, John Jenkins, Cliff W.T. Jones, Binnie McNeil, Billy J. Davies, Herbert Colwill, Archie Evans, Haydn Brew, Oswald Thomas, Cyril Emery.

A Steel Company of Wales coach outing in the 1960s. Included in the group, from left to right: Megan Williams, Dick Davies, Sister Anne Heycock, Binnie McNeil, Myrddin James, Les Richards, Winnie Morgan, Percy Hopkins, Lulu Haines.

Young Fred Roddis (about 14 years old) in his newly purchased top hat and tails, preparing his act ready to perform with the Trixie Reed Troop in the 1930s. The photograph was taken in the back garden of Fred's home in Velindre with Violet (left) and Gladys (who became a mayoress of Port Talbot, right). The Trixie Reed Troop was a very popular entertainment group and on this occasion was performing in the Working Men's Club in Talbot Square. The future Mrs Margaret Roddis went to see the show three times because she had taken a fancy to young Fred. She did not realise until many years after that the Fred she had married and Fred the performer were one and the same person!

The *Gypsy Baron*, as performed by the Port Talbot & District Amateur Operatic Society in the Margam College of Further Education, April 1957.

The Taibach and Port Talbot Temperance Brass Band, 1906.

Angharad Evans, shown here playing her Classarch harp, 1997. The 'Tree of Life' motive on the harp was designed and painted by her grandfather C. Des Tyler, an artist in his own right who has won prizes in a number of Steel Company of Wales/British Steel arts competitions. Angharad is one of only a few dozen triple harpists in the United Kingdom and she has a string of successes to her name having won the 12–15 group at the National Eisteddfod in Ebbw Vale in 1990 – the first time a triple harp had been played on a competitive stage for 70 years – and at Llandeilo in 1996 (solo 15–19). In 1997, at the Bala National Eisteddfod, Angharad won the open folk instrumental solo on the triple harp and also took third prize in the over-19 solo competition playing both the pedal and triple harp.

A scene from the pageant, held at Margam Park in 1933, to raise funds in aid of the Kenfig-Margam District Nursing Association. This photograph shows the principals in the Gretna Green wedding which was one of the attractive features of the pageant. Viscountess Pollington is seen as the abbess in white. From left to right: -?-, -?-, -?-, Katie Thomas (Stormy Farm), Miss O. Mort (daughter of Wilf Mort, chauffeur to E.V. David), W.J. Thomas (Old Park), M. Thomas, K. Thomas (Old Park), the Viscountess, E.V. David, Mrs E.V. David, -?-, J. Milton (who played the part of the blacksmith).

Another scene from the pageant held in Margam Park in June 1933, depicting the blacksmith (J. Milton) signing the register at the Gretna Green wedding of the young squire of Kenfig (W.J. Thomas) and Annie (Miss M. Thomas).

The Picturedrome

The Picturedrome (known to its regulars as the 'Cach'), Taibach, in the late 1940s. Originally the Workers' Hall, it was converted to a cinema in 1912. Films were again shown here in 1986 when the Picturedrome re-opened its doors after a lapse of twenty years. Its doors have now been closed for good, however.

The Majestic Cinema, Bethany Square, January 1986. In the heyday of cinema-going, Aberavon, Port Talbot, Taibach, and Cwmavon all had their fair share of cinemas. Alas, those days have now gone, with only the Plaza cinema in Port Talbot remaining. The Majestic, which had been empty and disused for many years, was eventually pulled down in 1996 to make way for a new shopping development; its demise signalled the end of an era.